May you
never forget no matter
how dark things seem you
have an eternal hope through
Jesus Christ and that you are
greatly loved.

*T*his journal belongs to

......................................................

*Hope*

© 2010 Ellie Claire™ Gift & Paper Corp.
www.ellieclaire.com

Compiled by Barbara Farmer
Designed by Lisa and Jeff Franke

Scripture references are from the following sources: The Holy Bible, New International Version®
NIV®. © 1973, 1978, 1984 by International Bible Society. Used by permission of Zondervan.
The New King James Version (NKJV). Copyright © 1982 by Thomas Nelson, Inc. Used by
permission. The Holy Bible, New Living Translation® (NLT). Copyright © 1996, 2004.
Used by permission of Tyndale House Publishers, Inc., Wheaton, Illinois. The Message
© 1993, 1994, 1995, 1996, 2000, 2001, 2002 by Eugene Peterson. Used by permission
of NavPress, Colorado Springs, CO. The New Century Version® (NCV). Copyright
© 1987, 1988, 1991 by Thomas Nelson, Inc. Used by permission. All rights reserved.

ISBN 978-1-934770-58-0

Printed in China

# HOPE

...inspired by life

*S*tand outside this evening. Look at the stars. Know that you are special and loved by the One who created them.

𝒢ive thanks to the Lord because He is good. His love continues forever.... He made the sun to rule the day.... He made the moon and stars to rule the night. His love continues forever.

𝒫SALM 136:1, 8-9 NCV

*Tuck [this] thought into your heart today. Treasure it. Your Father God cares about your daily everythings that concern you.*

Kay Arthur

You saw how the Lord your God cared for you all along the way as you traveled through the wilderness, just as a father cares for his child.

DEUTERONOMY 1:31 NLT

So wait before the Lord. Wait in the stillness. And in that stillness, assurance will come to you. You will know that you are heard;...you will hear quiet words spoken to you yourself, perhaps to your grateful surprise and refreshment.

AMY CARMICHAEL

In the morning, O Lord, You hear my voice; in the morning
I lay my requests before You and wait in expectation.

PSALM 5:3 NIV

*L*ift up your eyes. Your heavenly Father waits to bless you—
in inconceivable ways to make your life what you never
dreamed it could be.

ANNE ORTLUND

I lift up my eyes to the hills—where does my
help come from? My help comes from the Lord,
the Maker of heaven and earth.

PSALM 121:1-2 NIV

*In those times I can't seem to find God, I rest in the assurance He knows how to find me.*

NEVA COYLE

We throw open our doors to God and discover at the same moment that He has already thrown open His door to us. We find ourselves standing where we always hoped we might stand— out in the wide open spaces of God's grace and glory.

ROMANS 5:2 THE MESSAGE

*I*n the presence of hope—faith is born. In the presence of faith, love becomes a possibility! In the presence of love—miracles happen!

*R*OBERT *S*CHULLER

So let's do it—full of belief, confident that we're presentable inside and out. Let's keep a firm grip on the promises that keep us going. He always keeps His word.

HEBREWS 10:23-24 THE MESSAGE

*Commit to hope. There's reason to! For the believer, hope is divinely assured things that aren't here yet! Our hope is grounded in unshakable promises.*

JACK HAYFORD

The Lord looks after those who fear Him,
those who put their hope in His love.

PSALM 33:18 NCV

*Have* confidence in God's mercy, for when you think He is a long way from you, He is often quite near.

THOMAS À KEMPIS

How good it is to be near God! I have made the
Sovereign Lord my shelter, and I will tell everyone
about the wonderful things You do.

PSALM 73:28 NLT

Hope is some extraordinary spiritual grace that God gives us to control our fears, not to oust them.

VINCENT MCNABB

*B*e strong and of good courage…; do not fear nor be dismayed, for the Lord God—my God—will be with you. He will not leave you nor forsake you.

1 CHRONICLES 28:20 NKJV

The God who created, names, and numbers the stars in the heavens also numbers the hairs of my head.... He pays attention to very big things and to very small ones. What matters to me matters to Him, and that changes my life.

ELISABETH ELLIOT

Are not two sparrows sold for a penny? Yet not one of them will fall to the ground apart from the will of your Father. And even the very hairs of your head are all numbered. So don't be afraid; you are worth more than many sparrows.

MATTHEW 10:29-31 NIV

*God's hand is always there; once you grasp it
you'll never want to let it go.*

From eternity to eternity I am God. No one can snatch anyone out of My hand. No one can undo what I have done.

ISAIAH 43:13 NLT

*W*e do not understand the intricate pattern of the stars in their courses, but we know that He who created them does, and that just as surely as He guides them, He is charting a safe course for us.

BILLY GRAHAM

From high in the skies God looks around.... God's eye is on those who respect Him, the ones who are looking for His love. He's ready to come to their rescue in bad times; in lean times He keeps body and soul together.

Psalm 33:13, 18-19 THE MESSAGE

*After winter comes the summer. After night comes the dawn. And after every storm, there comes clear, open skies.*

SAMUEL RUTHERFORD

Because of the Lord's great love we are not consumed, for His compassions never fail. They are new every morning; great is Your faithfulness.

LAMENTATIONS 3:22-23 NIV

*God came to us because God wanted to join us on the road, to listen to our story, and to help us realize that we are not walking in circles but moving toward the house of peace and joy.*

Henri J. M. Nouwen

*I will walk among you and be your God,
and you shall be My people.*

LEVITICUS 26:12 NKJV

You can trust God right now to supply all your needs for today. And if your needs are more tomorrow, His supply will be greater also.

My God shall supply all your need
according to His riches in glory.

PHILIPPIANS 4:19 NKJV

*You are a child of your heavenly Father. Confide in Him. Your faith in His love and power can never be bold enough.*

BASILEA SCHLINK

I pray that God, the source of hope, will fill you completely with joy and peace because you trust in Him. Then you will over-
flow
with confident hope through the power of the Holy Spirit.

ROMANS 15:13 NLT

*Always be in a state of expectancy, and see that you leave room for God to come in as He likes.*

OSWALD CHAMBERS

I wait for the Lord, my soul waits,
and in His word I put my hope.

PSALM 130:5 NIV

*Our assurance is not based upon our ability to conjure up some special feeling. Rather, it is built upon a confident assurance in the faithfulness of God. We focus on His trustworthiness and especially on His steadfast love.*

Richard J. Foster

The work of righteousness will be peace, and the effect of righteousness, quietness and assurance forever.

ISAIAH 32:17 NKJV

*Hope does not necessarily take the form of excessive confidence; rather, it involves the simple willingness to take the next step.*

STANLEY HAUERWAS

The fundamental fact of existence is that this trust in God, this faith, is the firm foundation under everything that makes life worth living. It's our handle on what we can't see.

HEBREWS 11:1 THE MESSAGE

Hope is definitely not the same thing as optimism.
It is not the conviction that something will turn out well,
but the certainty that something makes sense,
regardless of how it turns out.

Václav Havel

So we do not give up. Our physical body is becoming...weaker, but our spirit inside us is made new every day. We have small troubles for a while now, but they are helping us gain an eternal glory that is much greater than the troubles.

2 CORINTHIANS 4:16-17 NCV

All [God's] glory and beauty come from within,
and there He delights to dwell. His visits there are frequent,
His conversation sweet, His comforts refreshing,
His peace passing all understanding.

THOMAS À KEMPIS

Instead of worrying, pray. Let petitions and praises shape your worries into prayers, letting God know your concerns. Before you know it, a sense of God's wholeness, everything coming together for good, will come and settle you down.

PHILIPPIANS 4:7 THE MESSAGE

*Faith goes up the stairs that love has made and looks out of the windows which hope has opened.*

CHARLES H. SPURGEON

And now abide faith, hope, love, these three;
but the greatest of these is love.

1 CORINTHIANS 13:13 NKJV

*P*art of our job is simply to be.... Part of our job is to expect
that, if we are attentive and willing, God will "give us prayer,"
will give us the things we need, "our daily bread,"
to heal and grow in love.

*R*OBERTA *B*ONDI

$\mathcal{B}$e joyful. Grow to maturity. Encourage each other.
Live in harmony and peace. Then the God of
love and peace will be with you.

2 $\mathcal{C}$ORINTHIANS 13:11 NLT

*If* you have a special need today, focus your full attention on the goodness and greatness of your Father rather than on the size of your need. Your need is so small compared to His ability to meet it.

And God is able to make all grace abound toward you,
that you, always having all sufficiency in all things,
may have an abundance for every good work.

2 CORINTHIANS 9:8 NKJV

*You* are never alone. In your heart of hearts, in the place where no two people are ever alike, Christ is waiting for you. And what you never dared hope for springs to life.

BROTHER ROGER OF TAIZÉ

The Lord, He is the One who goes before you. He will be with you, He will not leave you nor forsake you.

DEUTERONOMY 31:8 NKJV

For I am bound with fleshly bands,
Joy, beauty, lie beyond my scope;
I strain my heart, I stretch my hands,
And catch at hope.

CHRISTINA ROSSETTI

*N*o wonder my heart is glad, and I rejoice.
My body rest in safety.

*P*SALM 16:9 NLT

This life is not all. It is an "unfinished symphony" ...with him who knows that he is related to God and has felt "the power of an endless life."

HENRY WARD BEECHER

For now we see in a mirror, dimly, but then face to face. Now I know in part, but then I shall know just as I also am known.

1 CORINTHIANS 13:12 NKJV

*Ah, Hope! what would life be, stripped of thy encouraging smiles, that teach us to look behind the dark clouds of to-day, for the golden beams that are to gild the morrow.*

Susanna Moodie

I will sing of Your power. Yes, I will sing aloud of
Your mercy in the morning; for You have been my
defense and refuge in the day of my trouble.

PSALM 59:16 NKJV

You are in the Beloved...therefore infinitely dear
to the Father, unspeakably precious to Him.
You are never, not for one second, alone.

Norman Dowty

Steep yourself in God-reality, God-initiative, God-provisions.
You'll find all your everyday human concerns will be met.
Don't be afraid of missing out. You're My dearest friends!
The Father wants to give you the very kingdom itself.

LUKE 12:31-32 THE MESSAGE

*Those who contemplate the beauty of the earth find reserves of strength that will endure as long as life lasts.... There is something infinitely healing in the repeated refrains of nature—the assurance that dawn comes after night, and spring after the winter.*

Rachel Carson

The Lord is good to everyone. He showers
compassion on all His creation.

PSALM 145:9 NLT

*God* wants us to approach life, full of expectancy that God is going to be at work in every situation as we release our faith in Him.

COLIN URQUHART

This resurrection life you received from God is not a timid, grave-tending life. It's adventurously expectant.... God's Spirit touches our spirits and confirms who we really are. We know who He is, and we know who we are: Father and children.

ROMANS 8:15-16 THE MESSAGE

*Hope sees the invisible, feels the intangible,
and achieves the impossible.*

So we fix our eyes not on what is seen, but on what is unseen.
For what is seen is temporary, but what is unseen is eternal.

2 CORINTHIANS 4:18 NIV

*Our words can promote growth by wrapping others in a cocoon of love and hope.*

GARY SMALLEY AND JOHN TRENT

*Your* love has given me great joy and encouragement,
because you...have refreshed the hearts of the saints.

*Philemon* 1:7 NIV

If you believe in a God who controls the big things,
you have to believe in a God who controls the little things.
It is we, of course, to whom things look "little" or "big."

ELISABETH ELLIOT

$\mathcal{E}$ye has not seen, nor ear heard, nor have entered
into the heart of man the things which God
has prepared for those who love Him.

1 CORINTHIANS 2:9 NKJV

God says to His children: Are you lonesome? Breathe out My name. Come to Me and I will be your friend. Are you sick? Come to Me for healing. Are you left out of things? Feeling rejected and pushed aside? Come home to Me.

ALICE CHAPIN

Are you tired? Worn out? Burned out on religion? Come to Me. Get away with Me and you'll recover your life. I'll show you how to take a real rest. Walk with Me and work with Me— watch how I do it. Learn the unforced rhythms of grace.

MATTHEW 11:28-29 THE MESSAGE

*Hold on, my child! Joy comes in the morning!*
*Weeping only lasts for the night....*
*The darkest hour means dawn is just in sight!*

GLORIA GAITHER

His anger lasts only a moment, but His kindness lasts for a lifetime.
Crying may last for a night, but joy comes in the morning.

PSALM 30:5 NCV

God Incarnate is the end of fear; and the heart that realizes
that He is in the midst, that takes heed to the assurance of
His loving presence, will be quiet in the midst of alarm.

*F. B. Meyer*

*I*'m proud to praise God.... Fearless now, I trust in God;
what can mere mortals do to me?

*P*SALM 56:10-11 THE MESSAGE

The love of the Father is like a sudden rain shower that will pour forth when you least expect it, catching you up into wonder and praise.

RICHARD J. FOSTER

The Lord gives me strength and makes me sing;
He has saved me. He is my God, and I will praise Him.
He is the God of my ancestors, and I will honor Him.

EXODUS 15:2 NCV

*Peace with* God brings the peace *of* God. It is a peace that settles our nerves, fills our mind, floods our spirit, and in the midst of the uproar around us, gives us the assurance that everything is all right.

BOB MUMFORD

I am leaving you with a gift—peace of mind and heart. And the peace I give is a gift the world cannot give. So don't be troubled or afraid.

JOHN 14:27 NLT

Those who live on the mountain have a longer day than those who live in the valley. Sometimes all we need to brighten our day is to rise a little higher.

S. J. BARROWS

You, O Lord, are a shield for me, My glory
and the One who lifts up my head.

PSALM 3:3 NKJV

*We* are not alone on our journey. The God of love who gave us life sent us [the] only Son to be with us at all times and in all places, so that we never have to feel lost in our struggles but always can trust that God walks with us.

*Henri J. M. Nouwen*

Whether you turn to the right or to the left, your ears will hear a voice behind you, saying, "This is the way; walk in it."

ISAIAH 30:21 NIV

The Lord doesn't always remove the sources of stress in our lives...but He's always there and cares for us. We can feel His arms around us on the darkest night.

JAMES DOBSON

Those who live in the shelter of the Most High
will find rest in the shadow of the Almighty.

PSALM 91:1 NLT

One step ahead is all I now can see,
but He who notes the sparrow's fall, He leadeth me.
Not only by the waters still my feet may tread,
but with my hand in His, I know that I am led.

ELLA B. DOXSEE

*He* lets me rest in green meadows;
He leads me beside peaceful streams.

PSALM 23:2 NLT

*The* Creator thinks enough of you to have sent Someone very special so that you might have life—abundantly, joyfully, completely, and victoriously.

I am the Gate. Anyone who goes through Me will be cared for.... A thief is only there to steal and kill and destroy. I came so they can have real and eternal life, more and better life than they ever dreamed of.

JOHN 10:10 THE MESSAGE

*S*hould we feel at times disheartened and discouraged, a simple movement of heart toward God will renew our powers. Whatever He may demand of us, He will give us at the moment the strength and courage that we need.

*F*RANÇOIS *F*ÉNELON

The Lord...said to me, "My grace is enough for you. When you are weak, My power is made perfect in you."... For this reason I am happy when I have...all kinds of troubles for Christ. Because when I am weak, then I am truly strong.

2 CORINTHIANS 12:8-10 NCV

*What a strange thing is memory, and hope; one looks backward, the other forward. The one is of today, the other is of tomorrow.*

GRANDMA MOSES

You who serve God, praise God! Just to speak
His name is praise! Just to remember God
is a blessing—now and tomorrow and always.

PSALM 113:1-2 THE MESSAGE

*Optimism is the foundation of courage.*
NICHOLAS MURRAY BUTLER

So be strong and courageous! Do not be afraid....
For the Lord your God will personally go ahead of you.
He will neither fail you nor abandon you.

DEUTERONOMY 31:6 NLT

*He who breathes into our hearts the heavenly hope, will not deceive or fail us when we press forward to its realization.*

L.B. COWMAN

*N*ow we hope for the blessings God has for His children.
These blessings, which cannot be destroyed or be spoiled
or lose their beauty, are kept in heaven for you.

1 *P*ETER 1:4 NCV

*In* difficulties, I can drink freely of God's power and experience His touch of refreshment and blessing—much like an invigorating early spring rain.

What joy for those whose strength comes from the Lord....
When they walk through the Valley of Weeping,
it will become a place of refreshing springs.
The autumn rains will clothe it with blessings.

PSALM 84:5-6 NLT

When all my plans and hopes are fading like a shadow, when all my dreams lie crumbled at my feet, I will look up and know the night will bring tomorrow, and that my Lord will bring me what I need.

GLORIA GAITHER

*May* our Lord...encourage you and strengthen you in every good thing you do and say. God loved us, and through His grace He gave us a good hope and encouragement that continues for-ever.

2 *Thessalonians* 2:16 NCV

*The uncertainties of the present always give way to the enchanted possibilities of the future.*

GELSEY KIRKLAND

*We* set our eyes not on what we see but on what
we cannot see. What we see will last only a short time,
but what we cannot see will last forever.

2 Corinthians 4:18 NCV

*How could I be anything but quite happy if I believed always that all the past is forgiven, and all the present furnished with power, and all the future bright with hope.*

James Smetham

*W*e...wait with eager hope for the day when God
will give us our full rights as His adopted children.

*R*OMANS 8:23 NLT

*I believe that God is in me as the sun is in the color and fragrance of a flower—the Light in my darkness, the Voice in my silence.*

Helen Keller

*I* am the light of the world. He who follows Me shall
not walk in darkness, but have the light of life.

*J*OHN 8:12 NKJV

*When I need a dose of wonder I wait for a clear night and go look for the stars.... Often the wonder of the stars is enough to return me to God's loving grace.*

MADELEINE L'ENGLE

*P*raise be to the Lord, for He showed
His wonderful love to me.

*P*SALM 31:21 NIV

When life becomes difficult, when cracks spread through our existence and our strength seems to leak out, fill the gaps with hope. Like gold adorning distressed ancient art, hope will reinforce, add value, and reveal more beauty.

Barbara Farmer

*He* will give a crown of beauty for ashes, a joyous blessing
instead of mourning, festive praise instead of despair.

*Isaiah* 61:3 NLT

*Hope, like the gleaming taper's light,*
*adorns and cheers our way;*
*And still, as darker grows the night,*
*emits a lighter ray.*

OLIVER GOLDSMITH

Then your light will shine like the dawn, and your wounds
will quickly heal. Your God will walk before you,
and the glory of the Lord will protect you.

ISAIAH 58:8 NCV

*I believe that nothing that happens to me is meaningless, and that it is good for us all that it should be so.... As I see it, I'm here for some purpose.... In the light of the great purpose all our privations and disappointments are trivial.*

DIETRICH BONHOEFFER

*B*ut indeed for this purpose I have raised you up,
that I may show My power in you, and that
My name may be declared in all the earth.

*E*XODUS 9:16 NKJV

*God makes a promise—faith believes it, hope anticipates it, patience quietly awaits it.*

*Be* joyful in hope, patient in affliction,
faithful in prayer.

*R*OMANS 12:12 NIV

*If God, like a father, denies us what we want now, it is in order to give us some far better thing later on. The will of God, we can rest assured, is invariably a better thing.*

Elisabeth Elliot

*Yes, we should make the most of what God gives,*
*both the bounty and the capacity to enjoy it,*
*accepting what's given and delighting in the work.*
*It's God's gift! God deals out joy in the present, the now.*

ECCLESIASTES 5:19 THE MESSAGE

*Someday all you'll have to light the way will be a single ray of hope—and that will be enough.*

KOBI YAMADA

I pray that your hearts will be flooded with light so that you can understand the confident hope He has given to those He called—

His holy people who are His rich and glorious inheritance.

EPHESIANS 1:18 NLT

*K*nowest thou not that day follows night, that flood comes after ebb, that spring and summer succeed winter? Hope thou then! Hope thou ever! God fails thee not.

*C*HARLES *H*. *S*PURGEON

*E*verything He does reveals His glory and majesty.
His righteousness never fails.

*P*SALM 111:3 NLT

*Life is what we are alive to. It is not length but breadth....
Be alive to...goodness, kindness, purity, love, history,
poetry, music, flowers, stars, God, and eternal hope.*

Maltbie D. Babcock

Live in His presence in holy reverence, follow the road
He sets out for you, love Him, serve God, your God,
with everything you have in you.

DEUTERONOMY 10:12-13 THE MESSAGE

*God's promises are to be the guide and measure of our desires and expectations.*

MATTHEW HENRY

*D*elight yourself in the Lord and He will
give you the desires of your heart.

*P*SALM 37:4 NIV

The sunshine dancing on the water, the lulling sound of waves rolling into the shore, the glittering stars against the night sky—all God's light, His warmth, His majesty— our Father of light reaching out to us, drawing each of us closer to Himself.

*Every* good and perfect gift is from above,
coming down from the Father of the heavenly lights,
who does not change like shifting shadows.

*J*AMES 1:17 NIV

To believe in God starts with a conclusion about Him,
develops into confidence in Him, and then matures into
a conversation with Him.

Stuart Briscoe

Call to me and I will answer you. I'll tell you marvelous and wondrous things that you could never figure out on your own.

JEREMIAH 33:3 THE MESSAGE

*When the world around us staggers from lack of direction, God offers purpose, hope, and certainty.*

GLORIA GAITHER

Depend on the Lord in whatever you do,
and your plans will succeed.

PROVERBS 16:3 NCV

*Jesus Christ has brought every need, every joy, every gratitude, every hope of men before God. He accompanies us and brings us into the presence of God.*

DIETRICH BONHOEFFER

God said, "My presence will go with you.
I'll see the journey to the end."

EXODUS 33:14 THE MESSAGE

*God's love for me is ever the same. It is the one "constant" left in life today.*

*Jesus Christ is the same yesterday, today, and forever.*

HEBREWS 13:8 NCV

*Hope is faith holding out its hands in the dark.*
GEORGE ILES

*Your* word is like a lamp for my feet
and a light for my path.

PSALM 119:105 NCV

*If we will be quiet and ready enough, we shall find compensation in every disappointment.*

HENRY DAVID THOREAU

*W*ait for the Lord; be strong and take heart
and wait for the Lord.

PSALM 27:14 NIV

*I don't know, when I'm asking for something here on earth, what is going on in the innermost shrine of Heaven.... I am sure of one thing: it is good.... The hope we have is a living hope.... We wait for it, in faith and patience.*

ELISABETH ELLIOT

In my distress I cried out to the Lord; yes,
I cried to my God for help. He heard me from
His sanctuary; my cry reached His ears.

2 SAMUEL 22:7 NLT

*Love* means to love that which is unlovable, or it is no virtue at all; forgiving means to pardon that which is unpardonable, or it is no virtue at all—and to hope means hoping when things are hopeless, or it is no virtue at all.

*G. K. Chesterton*

You have this faith and love because of your hope, and what you hope for is kept safe for you in heaven.

COLOSSIANS 1:5 NCV

*Hope begins in the dark, the stubborn hope that if you just show up and try to do the right thing, the dawn will come.*

Anne Lamott

*I*f you spend yourselves in behalf of the hungry and satisfy the needs of the oppressed, then your light will rise in the darkness, and your night will become like the noonday.

*I*SAIAH 58:10 NIV

The God who flung from His fingertips this universe filled with galaxies and stars, penguins and puffins...peaches and pears, and a world full of children made in His own image is the God who loves with magnificent monotony.

BRENNAN MANNING

When I consider Your heavens, the work of Your fingers, the moon and the stars, which You have ordained, what is man that You are mindful of him, and the son of man that You visit him?

PSALM 8:3-4 NKJV

*We* have to realize that life finds us living every day with the unanswered and the unresolved. Faith helps us to live with the unanswered. Hope helps us to live with the unresolved. Trust helps us to accept...and go on with the work of living.

*Mark Connolly*

Know also that wisdom is sweet to your soul; if you find it, there is a future hope for you, and your hope will not be cut off.

Proverbs 24:14 NCV

*Trust is giving up what little I have in strength and power so I can confidently relax in His power and strength.*

GLORIA GAITHER

*My* soul finds rest in God alone;
my salvation comes from Him.

PSALM 62:1 NIV

*W*hen you accept the fact that sometimes seasons are dry and times are hard and that God is in control of both, you will discover a sense of divine refuge, because the hope then is in God and not in yourself.

CHARLES R. SWINDOLL

The Lord wants to show His mercy to you. He wants to rise and comfort you. The Lord is a fair God, and everyone who waits for His help will be happy.

ISAIAH 30:18 NCV

*H*ope is a state of mind, not of the world. Hope...is not the same as joy that things are going well, or willingness to invest in enterprises that are obviously heading for success, but rather an ability to work for something because it is good.

*V*ÁCLAV *H*AVEL

*H*e who has begun a good work in you will
complete it until the day of Jesus Christ.

Hope is not a granted wish or a favor performed; no, it is far greater than that. It is a zany, unpredictable dependence on a God who loves to surprise us out of our socks.

MAX LUCADO